Every Dollar Makes a Difference

Danica Kassebaum

Reader Consultants

Jennifer M. Lopez, M.S.Ed., NBCT
Senior Coordinator—History/Social Studies
Norfolk Public Schools

Tina Ristau, M.A., SLMS
Teacher Librarian
Waterloo Community School District

iCivics Consultants

Emma Humphries, Ph.D.
Chief Education Officer

Taylor Davis, M.T.
Director of Curriculum and Content

Natacha Scott, MAT
Director of Educator Engagement

Publishing Credits

Rachelle Cracchiolo, M.S.Ed., *Publisher*
Emily R. Smith, M.A.Ed., *VP of Content Development*
Véronique Bos, *Creative Director*
Dona Herweck Rice, *Senior Content Manager*
Dani Neiley, *Associate Content Specialist*
Fabiola Sepulveda, *Series Designer*

Image Credits: p.4, Brian Cassella/TNS/Newscom; p.5 Fabiola Sepulveda/TCM; p.12, 22 Alamy; p.16 Jonathan Wong/SCMP/Newscom; pp.20–21 Richard B. Levine/Newscom; p23 Comedy Kids/pp.24–25 Alamy/ZUMA Press; all other images from iStock and/or Shutterstock

Library of Congress Cataloging-in-Publication Data

Names: Kassebaum, Danica, author.
Title: Every dollar makes a difference : please give / Danica Kassebaum.
Description: Huntington Beach, CA : Teacher Created Materials, [2021] | Includes index. | Audience: Grades 2-3 | Summary: "Do you want to make a difference but do not know how? That is what fundraising is all about! Let's learn how to lead to a great event"-- Provided by publisher.
Identifiers: LCCN 2020043572 (print) | LCCN 2020043573 (ebook) | ISBN 9781087605036 (paperback) | ISBN 9781087619958 (ebook)
Subjects: LCSH: Fund raising--Juvenile literature. | Money-making projects for children--Juvenile literature.
Classification: LCC HV41.2 .K37 2021 (print) | LCC HV41.2 (ebook) | DDC 658.15/224--dc23
LC record available at https://lccn.loc.gov/2020043572
LC ebook record available at https://lccn.loc.gov/2020043573

TCM Teacher Created Materials
5482 Argosy Avenue
Huntington Beach, CA 92649-1039
www.tcmpub.com

ISBN 978-1-0876-0503-6

Printed in Malaysia.THU001.47741

Table of Contents

Every Little Bit Helps

Do you want to help someone in need? Do you want to make a difference? Maybe you are not sure what to do. That is what **fundraising** is all about. It is about raising money to make a change in the world. Every little bit helps!

Kids run to **raise** money for their school.

Jump into Fiction

Change the World

Miss Bay's class was working on their morning assignment when Alex raised her hand.

"Miss Bay?" Alex asked.

"Yes, Alex," said Miss Bay.

"Some of us have been talking. We have an idea," she said. "You know how we have been collecting change in our Change the World jar since the beginning of the school year?"

"To help save the rainforest," added Miss Bay.

"Yeah," said Alex. "Could we give that money to a different cause?"

"Mellie had to leave her house," said Alex. "The wildfires got too close. We want to help other people who had to do the same. Our money can help until they can go home."

"Great idea!" cheered Miss Bay.

Back to Nonfiction

People walk to raise money for cancer research.

Choose a Cause

The first step in fundraising is to choose a **cause**. It might be wildlife or people in need. It can be a **charity** that is close to where you live. Or it can be a cause from across the world. It is important to help others. By helping, we can improve lives and even the world.

Think and Talk

What cause would you like to support?

Alex's Lemonade Stand Foundation

A little girl set up a lemonade stand. She wanted to help kids with cancer. She had cancer too. Now, lots of kids like this one set up stands to help.

Be sure to choose a cause that has special meaning to you. Then, you need to decide how to raise money. Bake sales or collecting change at school are good ways to start. There are many other ways to raise money too.

People meet at the start line of a fundraiser walk.

Spread the Word

Next, it is time to tell people about the event. There are many ways to spread the word. Be sure to use more than one way to tell people. You might make **flyers** or signs and post them. If the event is at school, tell other classes. For big events, contact a local news station. The station can help spread the word.

A kid is interviewed by a local news station.

Making signs helps spread the word.

Be sure to tell everyone you know. The more people who come, the more money you will raise. Be sure to let people know how the money will help your cause. This may encourage others to help too. People working together can make a big difference!

Kids work to bring attention to a cause.

People carry a banner to help raise money for animals.

Saving the Animals

Animals need help too. Some groups hold tours of their animal centers. Tours help tell people about their cause. Then, people may give money to help.

It's Go Time

On the day of the event, there are a few things to remember. The first is to stay **organized**. Make sure every helper has a job. And don't forget to tell people why you are raising money. Tell them about the cause. Tell them why it is important.

A volunteer organizes canned goods.

Think and Talk

How can you tell the people in the photos are helpers?

These women work at bake sale for Cookies for Kids' Cancer.

On event day, make sure to keep track of the money raised. The money will be needed when the event is over. No matter how much, the money raised will help a good cause. Keep this in mind!

Cookies for Kids' Cancer

Cookies for Kids' Cancer helps raise funds to research and cure childhood cancer. They hold fundraisers such as bake sales.

Money Counts

At the end of the event, add up how much money was raised. It is like a giant math problem! Share the total with those who came to the event. They will want to know how much money was raised. They will want to know they have helped make a difference.

Comedy Kids

Two third-grade boys started telling jokes for money. They wanted to raise money for a good cause. They raised $18,000! Now, they help other kids host their own fundraisers.

Think and Talk

How can giving back change the life of the giver?

We all have the power to change the world. Together we can make a difference. We can share with those less fortunate. We can help those in need. That is the purpose of fundraisers. No amount is too small. Every little bit helps. Giving back can change lives. It can even change our own.

Glossary

cause—a belief or idea that people help or support

charity—an organization or company that helps people in need

flyers—sheets of paper with information on them to advertise something

fundraising—the act of collecting money for a cause through an event or activity

organized—planned or put together

raise—to collect or earn money

Index

Saving Paws
Rescue, Inc
Best Friends
Strut
YOUR MUTT
bestfriends.org

Civics in Action

Having a fundraiser is a good way to help. It can make a difference. You can start by planning an event of your own!

1. Choose the cause you want to help.
2. Decide on an event to raise money.
3. Plan how you could let people know about your event.
4. With permission, go ahead and have your event!